Especially for:

My Sister, My Friend

Other Andrews McMeel Books
by Joan Walsh Anglund

BETWEEN FRIENDS

THE BRAVE COWBOY

COWBOY AND HIS FRIEND

THE COWBOY'S CHRISTMAS

COWBOY'S SECRET LIFE

A CHRISTMAS ALPHABET

THE CHRISTMAS CANDY BOOK

THE CHRISTMAS COOKIE BOOK

HAPPY BIRTHDAY

LOVE IS THE BEST TEACHER

THE JEWELS OF THE SPIRIT

A PATCHWORK OF LOVE

YOU ARE LOVED

...My Sister, My Friend...

Written and Illustrated by

joan walsh anglund

Andrews McMeel Publishing

Kansas City

My Sister, My Friend copyright © 2004 by Joan Walsh Anglund. All rights reserved. Printed in China. No part of this book may be used or reproduced in any manner whatsoever without written permission except in the case of reprints in the context of reviews. For information, write Andrews McMeel Publishing, an Andrews McMeel Universal company, 4520 Main Street, Kansas City, Missouri 64111.

ISBN: 0-7407-4676-6

04 05 06 07 08   WKT   10 9 8 7 6 5 4 3 2 1

Book composition by Kelly & Company, Lee's Summit, Missouri

ATTENTION: SCHOOLS AND BUSINESSES

Andrews McMeel books are available at quantity discounts with bulk purchase for educational, business, or sales promotional use. For information, please write to: Special Sales Department, Andrews McMeel Publishing, 4520 Main Street, Kansas City, Missouri 64111.

My Sister, My Friend

For my sister, Patsy

When I needed strength,
        you supported me.
When I needed wisdom,
        you instructed me.
When I needed courage,
        you inspired me.
When I needed comfort,
        you loved me.

You have been to me
    that dearest of beings:
        my sister, my friend!

We are sisters
           by birth
but friends
           by choice.

When one is little,
> a sister's arms
> are a safe place
>> in a large and scary world.

A sister means
> never having
>> to be alone.

A sister is interested
 in whatever is happening
  to you.

She is never "too busy"
  to listen,
 and to care.

A sister is someone
> who believes in you . . .
sometimes,
> more
> than you do
>> yourself.

A sister is someone
 you can trust
 with all your worries,
 and with all your dreams.

Your deepest secrets
 are safe
 with her.

A sister is a friend
> when all the world
>> has turned against you.

She'll stand by you
> through any trouble,
> and when it's over
>> she'll wipe away
>>> your tears
>> and help you
>>> to "begin" again.

Sometimes,
    between even the best
        of sisters,
there can be
    hurt feelings
    or rivalry.

But, though sisters
> may tease and bicker
>> between themselves,
when one of them
>> is threatened
> by someone else,
>> no two people
>>> can be closer!

A sister is someone
    with whom you shared
        every day of your
                childhood.

She is like you
        and yet different . . .
    a part of you,
        and yet her own
                separate self.

A sister is like a mirror
 in which you can see
  a part of yourself
   reflected.

She is a kindred spirit . . .
 a twin-soul,
  a second self.

Sisters have a special bond
    that strengthens their love.
They are part of the same place,
    the same time,
        the same family.

Sisters share the same memories,
                    the same history.
Their faces are alike,
              their ways are alike,
and their spirits were shaped
              by the same forces.

A sister is fun to be with.
 Sisters can be silly together,
  trying on funny hats
    and dress-up clothes
  or giggling about the crazy
   things they did together
   when they were younger . . .
  that no one else knows about!

Sisters are kind to each other,
    always ready to comfort.
There are days when the dark
    clouds hide the sunlight
        and we feel helpless
            and alone;
that is the time
        when sisters
           are closest.
Holding hands,
        they draw strength
           from one another
      and find new hope
           together!

A sister likes us
        just the way
                we are!
She doesn't expect
        or want us
     to be
       anything
           different.

A sister wants
　　　　what's best for you,
because,
　　　　more than anyone
　　　　　　　　　　else,
she knows how hard
　　　　　　you've tried.

When they are young,
 sisters live in their own
  private world
  of childhood.
It is a small world
 of coloring books
  and bedtime stories
  and baking cookies.

It is a cozy world
    of teddy bears
        and tea parties,
  of sharing dolls
      and toys
          and secrets.

In that special world
                of childhood,
   sisters are together
              in everything
                      they do.
Together,
     they discover the
              first crocus
                  of spring.

Together,
>they picnic by the brook
>>in summer.

Together,
>they carve pumpkins,
>>eat turkey and
>>>cranberries,
>>hide Christmas gifts,
>>>and listen
>>>>for sleigh bells.

For all the holidays
        and the birthdays,
for all the celebrations
        and the quiet everyday times,
for all the days of a lifetime,
    a sister is always there,
                beside you.

A sister makes your life
>> happier,
> just because
>> she's in it.
She's a part of everything
> you've ever known
>> or loved.

And even when you're
　　　　　far apart
a sister is still with you.
　　She is always
　　　　　　in your heart.

A sister
>   is God's precious gift
>   >   to you . . .
>   a gift
>   >   that lasts
>   >   >   your whole life
>   >   >   >   through!

A sister is forever!